Lacy Sunshine

Rory and Her Sweet Cream Friends Coloring Book
Volume 7

**Illustrated by
Heather Valentin**

©Heather Valentin. All Rights Reserved.
Personal Use Only. No Redistribution.

This Book Belongs To
_____

Made in the USA
San Bernardino, CA
09 March 2018